HELP!

It's An
Indoor
Recess
Day

HELP!

It's An Indoor Recess Day

Dori E. Novak

CORWIN PRESS, INC.
A Sage Publications Company
Thousand Oaks, California

For information:

Corwin Press, Inc.
A Sage Publications Company
2455 Teller Road
Thousand Oaks, California 91320
E-mail: order@corwinpress.com

Sage Publications Ltd.
6 Bonhill Street
London EC2A 4PU
United Kingdom

Sage Publications India Pvt. Ltd.
M-32 Market
Greater Kailash I
New Delhi 110 048 India

Printed in the United States of America

Library of Congress Cataloging-in-Publication Data

Novak, Dori E.
    Help! It's an indoor recess day/by Dori E. Novak.
        p. cm.
    ISBN 0-7619-7527-6 (cloth: alk. paper)
    ISBN 0-7619-7528-4 (pbk.: alk. paper)
    1. Recesses. 2. Play. I. Title
    LB3033.N68 2000
    372.12′44—dc21

This book is printed on acid-free paper.

00 01 02 03 04 05 10 9 8 7 6 5 4 3 2 1

Corwin Editorial Assistant: Catherine Kantor
Production Editor: Denise Santoyo
Editorial Assistant: Victoria Cheng
Typesetter/Designer: Marion Warren
Cover Designer: Oscar Desierto

Contents

Preface

For most classroom teachers, waking up to the sounds of rain pounding on the roof or waking to any other negative weather condition that doesn't result in the immediate cancellation of school sends a thundering signal to pull the covers over their heads. They might also begin groaning and muttering things about the plight of educators. What's the problem? Rain on the roof triumphantly signals the return of an age-old teacher misery: indoor recess!

Managing indoor recess has probably been a dreaded part of the elementary classroom teacher's job since the days of the one-room schoolhouse. Yet education methods classes and classroom management courses rarely mention this ancient teacher trial. As every surviving teacher knows, managing indoor recess can take more teacher energy, patience, creativity, and skill than implementing the rest of the day's lesson plans. Sounds crazy, doesn't it? Yet most teachers would respond, "You just have to be there to believe it!"

I have tried to explain this innocent-sounding phenomenon to "outsiders" by asking them to imagine being the sole adult in charge at a birthday party for 35 bouncing, curious, exuberant children. I ask them to imagine the children have just been let loose in a room filled with toys right after they have been forced to sit quietly (mostly in one spot) and asked to read, write, and listen to an adult talk for about 3½ hours. Now they have the picture. To that, most just respond, "Why?" Perhaps I should answer that painting this picture is one way we educators ensure there will always be a shortage of teachers.

I am proud to offer this book, *Help! It's an Indoor Recess Day*. Most of the ideas found within were invented out of necessity as part of my own survival needs as a classroom teacher. Many were thought of years later as part of my staff development work with hundreds of teachers, both new and experienced. Although our experience differed, our goal was the same: Slay the old dragon of indoor recess management.

It is my great hope that you will find the ideas, activities, and strategies contained in this book to be inspirational and the ideas adaptable to your own classroom. Most of all, I hope you will experience the same delightful surprise I did: Tackled in a proactive way, with a positive attitude and a little help from your friends, the traditional noontime indoor recess can be great fun and a safe place to work out many of the challenges of classroom management. It is also an opportunity for us to demonstrate to our students that we haven't forgotten what it is like to have fun at play.

Who Will Enjoy Reading This Book?

Help! It's an Indoor Recess Day was written primarily for new and experienced teachers or teacher assistants wishing to develop or fine-tune their management skills while reducing their frustrations about classroom control. The book would be a valuable resource to anyone seeking to assist, instruct, mentor, or coach teachers, student teachers, assistants, and classroom volunteers in the management of indoor recess time. Many of the techniques and strategies described in the book transfer readily to the organization and management of high activity-oriented classrooms such as special education classes, gifted and talented classes, and developmental reading programs.

Instructional leaders such as principals, assistant principals, curriculum supervisors, staff developers, student teacher supervisors, and volunteer coordinators will enjoy the practical and innovative ideas found in this book. Finally, college instructors teaching about effective classroom management will find a wealth of information to support the value of advance planning, time management, and the accommodation of a variety of learning styles. The book will also interest all those wishing to understand or create motivating classroom environments that promote student responsibility and good decision making.

What Can You Expect to Find?

If *Help! It's an Indoor Recess Day* achieves the author's goal, once read, it will be flung aside by the enthusiastic reader who will race out searching for a classroom in which to implement the vast collection of ideas and easy-to-implement strategies described within.

In Chapter 1, the reader is invited to "roll up his or her sleeves" and take a good hard look at the present situation. To help with assessment and encourage objectivity, a checklist is provided. The strengths and weaknesses of the present classroom design are analyzed, and a plan begins to emerge. The reader learns how to maximize the space to accommodate the mobile bins that will be used in this approach.

In Chapter 2, the reader is encouraged to "take heart," no matter how frustrated he or she may have been in the past, and to consider a new way to look at the situation. The philosophical foundations for the new plan are laid.

In Chapter 3, the "four-corners approach" to managing indoor recess is introduced. It includes step-by-step guidelines for the design of the action plan and for the gathering of equipment and materials that will result in an efficient new way to organize free play.

In Chapters 4, 5, and 6, the reader learns how to accommodate different play styles and interests of children by creating special areas that are stocked with rainy-day activities for engrossing games, creative pursuits, and quiet activities that will keep the students engaged and delighted for 20 to 30 minutes.

In Chapter 7, the reader learns about a special area of the room called the "time-out corner," where children who have temporarily lost control of themselves can regain composure with dignity.

In Chapter 8, the reader learns how the teacher moves from "ready, to set, and finally, to go!" The reader learns how to carefully introduce the new system to the anxiously waiting students, monitor the implementation, and correct any problems. The goal is for the children to be able to enjoy safe and independent play that is followed by a smooth cleanup and readiness for the afternoon's activities.

In Chapter 9, the reader is given a baker's dozen of ideas for additional activity areas, along with suggestions for their location, setup, and use.

In Chapter 10, the reader takes a more in-depth look at what it takes to keep the system fresh and fun over time.

The book concludes with some final thoughts.

In summary, the book offers a unique opportunity for teachers to learn how to set up and take down a wonderful temporary playroom that clearly demonstrates that they understand the child's special world of play.

Special Thanks

I would like to thank the many teachers, friends, and administrators who have attended my classroom management workshops over the years. I am also grateful to my adventurous former students who not only agreed to test idea after idea but who also joined in on the inventing side with myriad creations of their own.

I would specifically like to express appreciation to Alice Foster, my editor at Corwin Press, who encouraged me to submit the proposal for this book. In addition, I am grateful to the following friends and colleagues:

Barbara Wolniak and Sue Gershman, instructional assistants at Waterloo Elementary School, in Howard County, Maryland;

Kari Premosicz, teacher at Burtonsville Elementary School, in Montgomery County, Maryland;

Sandy Finck, classroom teacher at Swansfield Maryland, Columbia, Maryland; and finally, to my friend and fellow author, Joanne Wachter, for her enthusiasm and unfailing support.

The contributions of the following reviewers are also gratefully acknowledged:

Janice M. Bibik, Associate Professor
Department of Health & Services—CSB, University of Delaware
Newark, Delaware

Kathryn McNaughton, Assistant Professor
Faculty of Education, University of Regina
Regina, SK Canada

Judith Olson, Instructional Services Consultant
Lakeland Area Education Agency 3
Cylinder, Iowa

About the Author

Dori E. Novak has been an educator for 28 years. She currently directs the Office of Staff Development and manages a nationally recognized staff development center for the Howard County public school system in Maryland. The center draws more than 40,000 clients and visitors each year.

Ms. Novak has 13 years of elementary classroom teaching experience in Grades 1 through 5, including 3 years of experience as a reading specialist. She also worked as an adjunct instructor for Western Maryland College, where she developed and taught a course on creative classroom management. This highly rated course was the first in the area to be entirely devoted to the topic of classroom management.

In addition, Ms. Novak is an accomplished speaker and consultant to education, government, and business on topics such as strategic planning and leadership development. She also assists organizations with comprehensive program planning and facilitation. Her clients have included the following: Maryland Instructional Television, Columbia Festival for the Arts, Griffith Oil Company, Howard County Community Health Foundation, Howard County Government, The Challenge Schools Program, and Towson University. She has consulted for groups such as Goddard Space Flight Center on creative problem solving. She has presented at Mount St. Mary's College, Loyola College, University of Maryland, and the National Staff Development Council. Her writing accomplishments include several nationally published articles and a book titled, *You Don't Have to Dread Cafeteria Duty* (1998), which was coauthored with Joanne C. Wachter.

Ms. Novak received her Bachelor of Arts degree from the University of Maryland and her Master of Science degree from Johns Hopkins University. She currently resides with her husband, Mike, in Ellicott City, Maryland.

This book is dedicated to my
patient and encouraging husband, Mike,
who never loses his sense of humor,
and to our five children:
Michael, Rob, Jennifer, Teresa, and Emily,
who have all suffered many indoor recesses.

1

Roll Up Your Sleeves! We're Going In!

The Challenge of Indoor Recess

What is the problem with indoor recess, anyway? It rains or snows and children stay indoors for about 30 minutes, entertain themselves, and then the afternoon continues as usual. Right? Most likely, both the children and the teacher are looking forward to the noontime break. Therefore, we need to consider that indoor recess usually begins as a disappointment for most children and teachers. The teachers need the time to recharge their batteries for the afternoon's activities. The children are looking forward to free play, fewer rules, and the chance to yell, scream, sing, dance, and laugh out loud—in short, fairly unlimited physical activity! Now it is not going to happen for either one the way they had imagined. Our task is to create a pleasing alternative that will be a win for both parties.

Take a Deep Breath and Observe the Present State

Before we can do things differently, we must first take a long, hard look at the present situation. Is there a specific plan for dealing with indoor recess? If not, we need one. If so, how is it working? What needs to be improved? Who are the children? How many are there? What are their ages, backgrounds, gender, interests, special talents, and needs?

Although this may sound like a barrage of questions, it is a very important first step if the resulting plan is to meet the specific needs of your class. We will be able to gather the information quickly and easily using the specially designed assessment on the next page. As you can imagine, the information we gain from the assessment will be vital for developing a truly customized plan for meeting the needs of your classroom.

The Big Picture

We can gain all the information we need about the present situation from the assessment plan below. The following key categories of information are helpful:

1. The results from the 12-point "Indoor Recess Assessment"

2. The analysis of potential trouble spots based on four key components

3. A profile of the children in your class

4. A sketch of your present classroom floor plan

Given the above information, we can sail along and introduce you to what I hope will be some exciting new ideas about managing indoor recess time.

As you use the Indoor Recess Assessment to examine the current situation, don't worry if you discover that some pieces are missing. After all, if you were perfectly satisfied with the way things are working now, you probably wouldn't be reading this book.

Indoor Recess Assessment

Your first step is to assess your current state using Table 1.1.

TABLE 1.1   Indoor Recess Assessment Checklist

Directions: Observe a typical indoor recess period and indicate, with a numerical score, the extent to which each of the following is presently occurring. Use the following 5-point scale: 1 = *poor*, 2 = *fair*, 3 = *acceptable*, 4 = *good*, 5 = *super*.

_____ 1. There are adequate places to play that include a quiet area.
_____ 2. Space is designated for a creative area (preferably near a sink).
_____ 3. Space is designated for action play that doesn't interfere with the quiet area.
_____ 4. There is a special "get-away" or time-out area that will accommodate one person.
_____ 5. There is an adequate supply of activities reserved only for indoor recess time.
_____ 6. Games and activities are appropriate for the ages and interests of all students.
_____ 7. There is an adequate variety of quiet, creative, and action games and activities.
_____ 8. Agreed-on standards for conduct are written in large print and clearly posted.
_____ 9. Children appear to know what to do to begin the recess time.
_____10. There is demonstrated understanding of cleanup and closure responsibilities.
_____11. Children use effective, independent procedures for getting drinks and using lavatories.
_____12. Effective, unobtrusive methods are used by the teacher for reducing noise levels.

Next, add your total score from Table 1.1. Then, find it on the appropriate line in Table 1.2. This score will give you a general idea of how things are currently during indoor recess.

TABLE 1.2   Interpreting Your Scores

If your score is

55-60	Give this book to a friend or become a coach to someone who needs support.
44-54	Congratulations, great things are already happening. Use the book to fine-tune.
33-43	"Bravo!" for recognizing the need for new solutions. Charge on!
0-32	Hats off to you for having the courage to look! Now, let's go after the dragon!

What's Working, What's Not?

Congratulations! Now that you have a general score and a rough appreciation of the current state, let's look more closely at some specific areas that could use a little boost. By the way, these same assessment tools can be used later to help you see progress and identify lingering problems. They can also provide an excuse for some celebration.

Identifying Possible Trouble Spots

Using Table 1.3, you can determine specific trouble spots by analyzing your indoor recess scores according to the following key areas: the physical arrangement of space, guidelines for student behavior, adequacy of games and activities, and efficacy of the management system.

These assessment tools can help you to establish baseline data at the beginning of the program, mid-point improvements, and final results.

TABLE 1.3   Identifying Classroom Trouble Spots

Directions: Add the line scores from the Indoor Recess Assessment (see Table 1.1), as indicated below, to get a total for each of the four main areas. The maximum score for each area is 15 points.

1. Physical arrangement of classroom space _____
    (add lines 1, 2, 3)
2. Guidelines for student behavior _____
    (add lines 4, 8, 12)
3. Adequacy of games and activities _____
    (add lines 5, 6, 7)
4. Efficacy of the management system _____
    (add lines 9, 10, 11)

Analyzing the Results

At this point, we have some baseline data and a rough idea regarding possible trouble spots or areas of greatest need. This information will be very helpful as you design a program that will fit the specific needs of your students. You can also use this same assessment process to evaluate progress 6 to 8 weeks from now. When you get close to having 15 points in each area, indoor recess should be a joy, and you will be free to tackle some other classroom challenge.

Who Are the Children?

The third category of data you will need is a profile of the children the program is being designed to serve. As you know, for any classroom plan to be successful, you need to consider the needs, interests, and age levels of the children it is being designed to serve. A recess plan is no different. It is helpful to look at the children as a group as well as individuals.

The Children as a Group

This information can usually be derived from observations and a review of student records.

1. How many children are in the class?

2. What is the breakdown in terms of gender?

3. What is the breakdown in terms of race?

4. What is the breakdown in terms of ethnicity?

5. How many students have special needs?

6. Have you made other general observations that need consideration?

The Children as Individuals

This information can usually be derived from personal interviews, observations, and surveys.

1. What are the children's favorite hobbies, books, TV and movie characters, sports, kinds of music, games, and activities?

2. What three things would they most love to do that would be appropriate for indoor recess?

3. What ideas or suggestions do the children have for a great indoor recess that would be safe, considerate of others, and easy to set up and clean up in about 20 minutes?

4. What do they think would be fair standards of behavior that everyone should follow?

Considering the Classroom Floor Plan

The fourth and final category of information you need to evaluate your present situation is a sketch of the classroom. Because the same physical space is usually used for both classroom instruction and indoor recess, the design of the space is very important. As a former classroom teacher, I realize that one criterion for a successful indoor recess plan is that it is not disruptive to the regular classroom instructional program that usually follows immediately after indoor recess. You must be very clever to design the indoor system so that it can appear and disappear as if by magic! What a challenge!

A Look at the Current Floor Plan

Make a detailed sketch of your current classroom. Be sure to include the following: storage areas, sinks, tiled areas, location of chalkboards, bookshelves, doors, windows, placement of learning centers, activity areas, electrical outlets, desks, furniture, and anything else that you think might pertain to the design of the indoor recess project (e.g., computer stations). This information will be very helpful as you plan placements for the exciting activity areas to come. Figure 1.1 is an example of a classroom arranged for activity centers.

8

Figure 1.1. An Example of a Classroom Setup for Indoor Recess

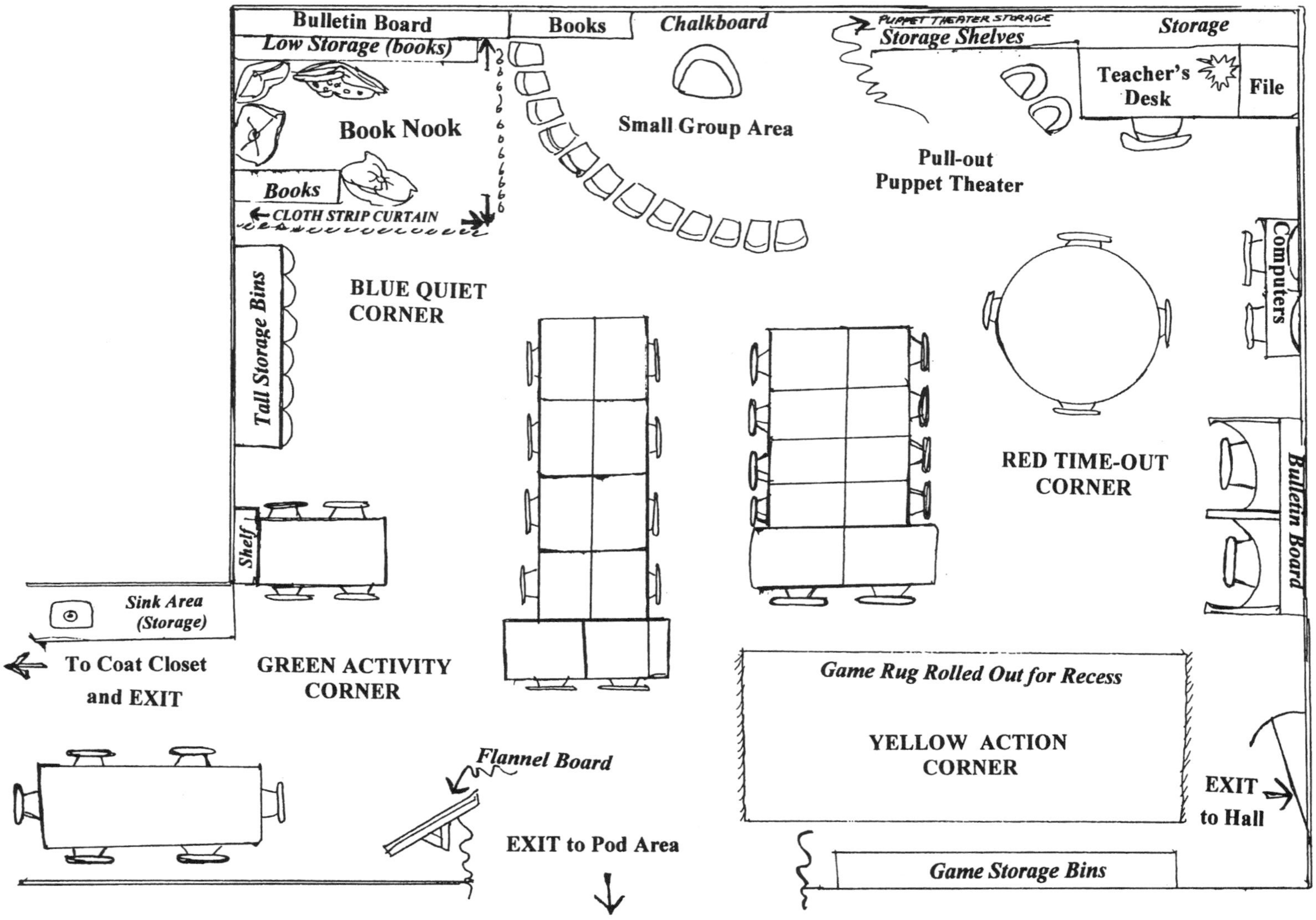

Storage

Teacher's Desk

File

Computers

Bulletin Board

EXIT to Hall

PUPPET THEATER STORAGE
Storage Shelves

Pull-out
Puppet Theater

RED TIME-OUT
CORNER

Chalkboard

Books

Small Group Area

Game Rug Rolled Out for Recess

YELLOW ACTION
CORNER

Game Storage Bins

Bulletin Board

Low Storage (books)

Book Nook

CLOTH STRIP CURTAIN

Books

BLUE QUIET
CORNER

Tall Storage Bins

Flannel Board

EXIT to Pod Area

Shelf

GREEN ACTIVITY
CORNER

Sink Area
(Storage)

To Coat Closet
and EXIT

2

Take Heart!

There Is Another Way to Look at This

Setting the Stage

At this point, you may be wondering why you have been asked to spend so much time observing and analyzing the physical arrangement of the entire classroom when all you want to know is how to make life a little easier during periods of indoor recess. Good question!

Because we are talking about the same children, same space, same equipment, and most likely the same teacher, the management system used for one is bound to affect the other. This can be great news. If you decide to implement the recess management plan, your energy and effort will be doubly rewarded with many benefits to regular classroom instruction time as well. For instance, the same standards of conduct apply in both cases, and the diverse activity areas will accommodate different learning styles as well as play styles.

Imagine This Scene: The Indoor Recess Plan in Action

It is one of those rainy days at school. Ms. Miller's third-grade class has just finished the morning's activities, and everyone is getting ready for lunch. She reminds the class that today there will be an indoor recess. She pulls out a colorful poster with the following title: Indoor Recess Agreements. The teacher attaches the poster to the board and reminds everyone that they have agreed to abide by the five class standards. Because this is still a new program, one student volunteers to read the agreements.

Indoor Recess Agreements

I agree to:

1. Use an indoor voice

2. Walk, not run

3. Put away each activity as it is used

4. Be considerate of others

5. Be cleaned up and in my seat by the end of the Lone Ranger theme

The children laugh at the last line, remembering the fun of scurrying around to be the first table ready for the afternoon.

The teacher displays one more poster. This time it is a puzzle featuring a tangram fox. The students recall the routine. They know the location of the plastic bin that houses the tangram puzzles. If they feel like taking on today's challenge, they can try making the figure at their desks. If they are successful, they can write their names on the laminated poster for a class cheer at the end of recess. This activity is described in detail in Chapter 8.

Transforming the Classroom for Indoor Activity Time

The teacher catches the eye of this month's three recess monitors who are already in line for lunch. They have completed their task of bringing out several color-coded boxes and have placed them in the appropriate activity areas. Because these games and activities are reserved just for indoor playtime, they seem like a special treat. That completes the recess transformation. The children get in line for lunch. Some are already puzzling, "Which tangram piece could make a fox's nose?"

Launching the Action

When the children return to the classroom, everyone immediately takes a seat at their desk, and a temporary quiet falls over the class. They know the teacher will dismiss them quickly by tables. The dismissal pattern will vary, but within a few seconds, the children will have elected to play in the Yellow Action Corner, the Green Creativity Corner, the Blue Quiet Zone, or to remain at their desks for now.

Each area is posted with a large numeral that reminds everyone of the corner's capacity. If the corner is full, children choose another alternative. Because there is a wealth of options, no one seems to mind. The 20 minutes will go quickly. The children have learned the efficacy of gaining the most playtime by selecting and staying in one area for all or most of the recess. Some notice the refrains of soft background music. The teacher is aware that this subtle addition creates a unique atmosphere for the recess time that will help with the transformation back to classroom instruction when recess is over.

Returning the Calm

After about 20 minutes, a few children hear the soft "ding" of a timer. Then, everyone in the class notices the refrains of the now-familiar Lone Ranger's theme (from *The William Tell Overture*) indicating that cleanup time has begun. Everyone knows the music will gradually get louder as the time gets shorter. The music signals them (as opposed to the teacher trying to tell everyone) that they have about 3 minutes to come to closure on their activity, clean up, and get to their seats.

This feels like a game in itself. No one wants to lag behind when the music comes to the final crescendo. The music stops abruptly, and the class applauds their fast cleanup. As the teacher provides recognition for various accomplishments, any new records that have been set in the activity corner, and that day's puzzle champions, the three recess monitors quickly scan the classroom for any stray materials. They collect the activity boxes and return them to the storage area. Having accomplished their job, they return to their seats. The teacher smiles and nods appreciation. Indoor recess is now officially over, and the class is ready to hear an overview of the activities that are in store for them for the afternoon. Whew!

What Does It Take to Make This Scene a Reality?

The main ingredient for this program's success is advance preparation. This is not hard to do; in fact, most teachers would say it is great fun. But it is tough to find the time. Perhaps this is because most teachers invest their time in planning for the instructional program. This is both understandable and ironic. The irony is that without investing time in the proactive management of this essential classroom activity, the cost in teacher enthusiasm, morale, and energy on every bad weather day is disproportionately grievous. On the other hand, teachers can take care of this challenge once and for all with the following easy-to-implement plan.

3

Introducing the "Four-Corners Approach" to Managing Indoor Recess

---

What Is the Four-Corners Approach?

The "four-corners approach" is a unique classroom management plan that capitalizes on children's natural "play styles" and preferences. It also addresses the teacher's need for an efficient approach to managing indoor recess that can be ready on a raindrop's notice. Once established, the program takes only a small amount of teacher energy to maintain.

The approach is based on the assumption that most teachers would be delighted if indoor recess:

- ▶ Keeps the children safely engaged and entertained for about 20 minutes
- ▶ Maintains a noise level that does not disrupt nearby classrooms or teachers

▶ Requires a minimum of teacher management

▶ Leaves the classroom neat and orderly for the afternoon's activities

Similarly, it is assumed that most children love recess and are willing to comply with a few reasonable rules and standards for behavior to get time to play. The most common problems that teachers face when managing indoor recess usually fall into the following categories:

1. Conflicts created because of space problems

2. Inadequate supply or inappropriate activity choices

3. Unclear or inconsistent expectations

4. Inefficient routines and management systems

The four-corners approach is carefully designed to support these assumptions, address the problems, and help you to set the stage for such great indoor playtimes that other teachers will want to come and watch!

What Does It Take to Set Up This System?

To set up this system, the teacher has to be willing to invest some time in proactive planning. This may sound tough to do. Teachers often feel overwhelmed and far too busy to give extra time to a "nonessential" such as indoor recess. Therefore, planning typically consists of locating a shelf in the classroom that can hold whatever games they can gather up and lump together. As for the rest of the plan, they will figure that out when it rains. This is entirely understandable. However, for the teachers who are willing to make a one-time, proactive investment, the reward will be an extra measure of classroom peace and satisfaction on every bad weather day for the rest of their teaching careers. Sounds like a pretty good investment, doesn't it? What's more, these teachers will find that the instructional time that follows recess will be far more productive.

Requirement 1: The Careful Arrangement of Space

A key component of the four-corners program is the arrangement of specially designated activity areas that are integrated right into the basic classroom floor plan. In fact, you can use the classroom floor plan that you sketched out in Chapter 1 to play along. You will probably find that you already have all or most of these areas in your present classroom design. If so,

Figure 3.1. Strive for the Careful Arrangement of Space

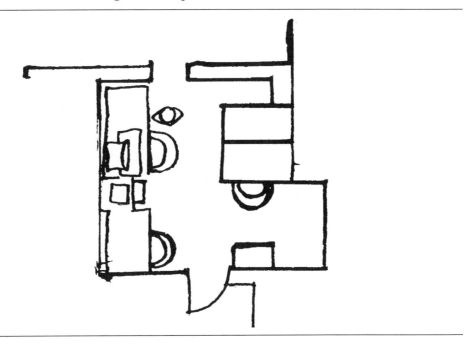

all the better. If not, you are in for a double treat because these same areas will address both play and learning activities. These versatile activity areas will enhance the regular instructional program during class time, and, when needed, the room can be transformed into a great indoor play area in about 4 organized minutes.

Why Do We Need to Designate Special Activity Areas?

You have probably witnessed the following common indoor recess scenes many times: A young student is engrossed in pushing a big truck across an imaginary trail. He bumps sharply into two students who are trying to read a story to each other. In another area of the room, a gigantic block tower falls over onto someone's origami project. Can you hear the noise?

Designating special areas of the classroom for activities that are similar is logical and efficient, and it can greatly reduce many of the common hazards of indoor recess. It also increases classroom harmony by localizing high-activity games in the safest and most spacious areas of the classroom. This allows the teacher to offer a wider range of play activities and tends to keep the interest of children longer. These special centers are also color-coded, which makes cleanup time easier.

What Are the Four Play Areas?

The "four corners" refer to the four activity areas prescribed for this program, which are:

1. A yellow action area for high-activity games (described in Chapter 4)

2. A green center for creative pursuits (described in Chapter 5)

3. A blue area for quiet activities that require more concentration (described in Chapter 6)

4. A red "time-away" corner (described in Chapter 7) for those who occasionally need a temporary "get-away" spot to regain their composure or self-control

Each area is given its own special color to aid in organizing the activities, storing the materials, and cleaning up the areas. Feel free to make up your own unique color scheme. Perhaps you already have some or all of these areas in your classroom. If not, and you wish to try this system, don't worry. The ensuing chapters will include everything you need to know to set up or enhance a high-functioning center program. You will also find a profile of the students most likely to be drawn to each area, a collection of activities, and some guidelines for getting started.

Requirement 2: An Impressive Supply of Age-Appropriate Games and Activities

The greatest indoor recess classrooms are generously stocked with a variety of games and activities that seem to magically appear just for indoor recess and then disappear at the end of it. The activities are arranged in an orderly manner that helps children to clean up in a hurry (almost always the case). Both the activities and containers are color-coded to match the color of the area. This makes it easier for the children to be neat and efficient. It is also wise to include a labeled "mystery box" where lost or unknown pieces can be collected.

How to Collect a Generous Supply of Games Without Much Cash

First, you probably already have a store of games and activities, so start there. Take inventory. Jot down what you have according to these basic play styles: action-oriented games, creative pursuits, and quiet activities. If you are coming up short, read on!

Locating Free or Inexpensive Games

There are a number of ways to build an impressive supply of games and activities, even if you have little or no money. The following list will provide some suggestions to get you started:

1. Prepare a letter to parents in one of the upper grades that asks for the donation of extra games to your classroom. Include suggestions.

2. Visit yard sales.

3. Prepare a list of requests and ask friends and family to keep an eye out for you.

4. Put a notice in the community paper.

5. Make game boards, puzzles, bingo cards, floor mats for hopscotch, and so on.

6. Ask the children to bring in games that are in good condition that they no longer want to play.

7. Ask Toys-R-Us or a local toy store for donations. (It makes a tax-deductible contribution and great advertising for them as well as a generous gift to your classroom.)

How to Become a Top-Notch Fundraiser for Your Classroom

What if you would like to have money for new or better games and you don't know of a source? When it comes to securing funding for projects, many teachers back off from a lot of their classroom dreams. They either assume there are no funds available (before they even ask) or do not use a thoughtful, professional approach to securing funding. Think about it for a moment. If you wanted money to support your program, who and how would you ask for it? The most logical approach for a classroom teacher to use is to ask the principal. This is a fine first step. However, teachers rarely think much about how best to approach the principal and are often too quick to take no for an answer.

Imagine this scene: The teacher catches the principal in the office and asks, "Could I please have some money to buy activities for a recess management program that I am working on?" The principal responds without looking up, "Sorry, don't have any." The teacher walks away feeling defeated and remembers an experienced colleague who predicted, "Go ahead and ask, you won't get any money."

The following seven steps will make it hard for your principal or anyone else, for that matter, to turn you down. However, keep in mind that the principal is not the only funding source around. Other sources include local rotary clubs, community groups, and business partnerships. These same seven steps can be applied in those situations too.

Seven Steps for Successful Fundraising

The first rule of fundraising is to think of the word *no* as just a signal that marks the end of Round 1 (much too soon to ever leave the ring!).

Instead of giving up at the first sign of resistance, experiment with the following strategies that are guaranteed to increase your chances for success, or at least your time in the ring:

1. Approach the search for funding with a light-hearted attitude. The task is not to go "begging for money" but to enlist others in helping you to find solutions for your funding problems. If it doesn't work, don't worry. For one thing, this book is going to give you lots of ideas for getting what you need without much money. However, it is also true that a mix of free materials and cold-hard cash couldn't hurt anything.

2. Put your request in writing. A written request looks more professional and serves as a reminder to the principal after you have gone. It also provides a document that you can refer to later.

3. Don't ask for money "on the fly." It appears frivolous. Make an appointment, bring in your written request, and present your case. Phrase your request as classroom equipment needed for recess activities—as opposed to "toys or games." These suggestions might seem more formal, but your request will be remembered longer, and (again) it will be easier to refer to the meeting in the future.

4. If the response to your request is no, try not to take it personally. Instead, listen attentively to the reason, summarize it back to the person so he or she can tell that you were really listening, and say something like, "I still want to find funding for this program. Do you have any suggestions that I could try?"

5. Throughout the conversation, keep a pleasant look on your face, and don't pout or get grumpy if you are not hearing good news just yet.

6. End with a sincere "thank you" and ask, "Do you mind if I ask you again in the future in case circumstances might have improved?"

7. Follow up the meeting with a brief note of thanks.

Now, congratulate yourself! The very least you have achieved is that your principal has been reminded that you are a brave, problem-solving teacher looking to improve your program for children. That is hardly a loss. You have also let it be known that you are not giving up.

Requirement 3: Clear and Consistent Standards

A vital piece of any classroom plan is a clear set of rules that everyone understands and agrees to support. You can call these rules, standards, expectations, agreements, the class creed, or whatever you like, but without them, the indoor recess system has little chance of succeeding. In fact, clear expectations may be even more vital for indoor recess because the free-play aspect probably requires more self-control from students than the more structured regular instructional time. Ironically, this extra freedom within the framework of ordered activities in the four corners improves the indoor recess period.

There are two things that most teachers will quickly agree on concerning classroom management: first, that clear and consistent standards of conduct are vital, and second, that it is extremely challenging and time-consuming to teach children about clear and consistent standards of conduct. We can make it a lot easier by having a plan. But we still need to take time to teach the children about the expectations and the routines.

Building a Positive Group Habit

Teaching children to conduct themselves in a certain way requires the intentional building of positive group habits. My experience is that we rarely do that. In fact, I suspect that most teachers who complain about the poor behavior of children or their lack of discipline have not specifically instructed the children in clear behavior expectations or have given up too soon. To teach positive class conduct, we have to get over the notion that children "should" come to school knowing how to behave and that we "shouldn't" have to teach it. Baloney! This attitude will only frustrate you.

For the most part, children do come to school knowing how to behave. They just choose not to, sometimes. Also, the definition of acceptable behavior varies greatly. You may think the children's behavior is deplorable. They may think it is great. It can be a tough challenge to get a room full of students with varying backgrounds to abide by the same standards. But it can happen. To succeed, you must have clear expectations and demonstrate strong, caring leadership on a consistent basis.

The task of building positive group habits is not as difficult as it sounds. In fact, it happens automatically every fall, starting with the first day of school. The trick is to assume the leadership role early so that you can direct which habits are being built. If you wish to create the safe and nurturing environment for learning and playing, you will need at least these three things: consistency, encouragement to the forgetters, and unwavering high expectations for all.

Five Tips for Establishing Standards for Self-Conduct

1. Select only a few key standards (no more than five).

2. State them positively and in the language of children.

3. Post them, using large, fat print (no cursive writing) on the wall in full view.

4. Discuss them with the class, communicate them to parents, and request everyone's help in supporting them until they become a class habit.

5. Teach them. This requires reviewing the standards for several days in a row (in the beginning). It also means having student's take turns reading them out loud, writing them in class journals, making posters for their notebooks, getting parents to sign that they have reviewed them, and perhaps signing a contract that they will support them. It sounds like a lot, but research tells us that learning takes about 35 repetitions for most people and then periodic reviews after that. This investment of time will pay off handsomely all year when the classroom functions like a dream (at least on most days).

An Example of Standards of Self-Conduct

The following is an example of a set of standards of behavior or agreements that comply with the requirements described earlier. You will notice that they are so simple that you might wonder if they could work. The simplicity and brevity of each statement are purposeful. Just imagine, if all the children in the class agreed to abide by these five simple standards, how peaceful and productive everyone's life in the classroom would be.

During indoor recess, I will:

1. Use an indoor voice

2. Walk, not run

3. Put away each game after it is used

4. Be kind to others

5. Be cleaned up and in my seat by the end of the Lone Ranger theme

Requirement 4: An Efficient Management System

The final component of the four-corners approach is the management system. This is the last piece of the puzzle, the key ingredient, the magic that makes it all work. Just imagine, with a mere signal from the teacher, an amazing automatic pilot of management can be set in motion. It is like watching a miracle in action. Awesome! The children may surprise you by their cooperation and willingness to follow routines and procedures. Most children appreciate structure and respond positively to the opportunity to manage their own behavior.

Some teachers find it hard to believe, but most children would rather do things right than have the teacher upset or angry with them. This requires that the children understand the expectations and that the expectations seem fair to them. All this can happen when they see that you are offering them the special treat of free activity time. For that they are even willing to abide by reasonable standards of conduct. All you have to do is be very clear regarding the expectations you have for them and make it possible for them to be successful.

In Chapter 8, we will look in depth at the automatic pilot system that will be designed to operate the program. But we aren't there yet. Right now, we need to get the activity centers set up and ready for business.

4

Launching the Yellow Action Corner

Let me stretch, move freely, get out of my seat.
I want to do something fun!

Who Is the Yellow Action Corner For?

The activity-oriented child is usually the easiest for the teacher to spot. In fact, before you read any more about this corner, you could probably jot down the names of several children from your class who would likely be drawn to this area. They are the charming, bouncy, exuberant children who look like they are being tortured when asked to "Sit still!" They are often loud, sometimes aggressive, move fast, usually quick to smile, laugh a lot, and seem to electrically charge the very air in the room around them. School can be a real challenge for them because they always seem to be in trouble. Parents shake their heads and teachers get frustrated. Often the quiet students want to stay far away from them.

What Do Action-Oriented Children Appreciate?

What the action-oriented child needs is a place to play that feels like it fits them. They need more elbowroom, more wiggle room, and a wide range of activities that give them a chance to exercise their arms and legs. This calls for some careful planning, for if these children's needs are not accommodated, it will be like trying to keep a lid on a box of monkeys for 20 to 30 minutes.

The Location and Setup

Look again at your classroom floor plan and locate a good spot for the action corner. Select the most open area of the classroom. Give it as much empty floor space as possible, and have a storage shelf nearby to hold the many game boxes and activities associated with action play. This area tends to have the bulkiest items to store such as Nerf basketball, cars, trucks, balls for rolling, floor mats for hopscotch, giant tic-tac-toe, exercise mats for sit-up challenges, chin-up bars fastened in the doorway, and tons of blocks for building. If space allowed, I have often thought that a couple of used, self-propelled treadmills would be a fabulous activity for this area. All the activities should be color-coded with yellow stickers.

Guidelines for Use

Having the action games located in one area protects the children who wish to concentrate on reading or doing puzzles. It also keeps the children who are drawing and creating from getting bumped. The four-corners approach discourages children from switching from center to center. However, if children want a change, they may elect to return to their desks, at any time, and do quieter activities such as read, draw, do a puzzle, or play a board game.

A Baker's Dozen of Activities and Ideas to Include in the Action Corner

1. *Make and fly a paper airplane.* This activity invites students to have a flight contest with a friend, try to set a record for distance, and then post the record on a classroom chart. To be able to offer this activity, students need a book (or chart) of directions for making paper airplanes. They also need a designated flight path that can be marked off by laying down a specially prepared piece of clothesline. You might want to pre-measure the line to indicate feet, use a tape measure to indicate the "flight take-off zone," and, to really add excitement, a couple of captain's hats. Finally, the students need a posted class record where they can record their successes and invite challengers.

2. *Roll a ball back and forth to a friend.* This may not sound like much of an activity at first, but given a designated area and some balls, children will invent their own games. Some include crash ball, race ball, and rolling dodgeball. A fun thing to add is a small set of bowling pins.

3. *Play hopscotch, indoor horseshoes, or ring toss.* All you need for this is a predesigned floor mat and the rings, rocks, or the horseshoes and posts.

4. *Play Nerf double basketball.* Directions: The ball must also land in a wastebasket. To offer this activity, inform students where the basket can be set up and provide the ball, the wastebasket, and perhaps a small clipboard to make keeping score more fun.

5. *Play board games, dominoes, or card games.* It is understandable that board games make up most of the classroom's recess collection. They are versatile, easy to store, easy to obtain, and fun to play again and again. Also, if you are short on space, they can be taken to desks as well as played on the floor.

6. *Set up a diorama with miniature figures.* Examples of scenes that are fun to set up include castle sets, a farm with barn and animals, an airport scene complete with planes and runway, and a space station.

7. *Arrange for chin-up challenges.* Metal extension bars are available for this, and it provides a great source of contained physical activity. The bar can be attached inside a doorway, and the students are set to break records.

8. *Play pick-up sticks or jacks.* These are two great old-fashioned, inexpensive games that take fine motor skills and patience. Better get more than one set of each.

9. *Put on a flannel board play or retell a story.* Materials required for this activity include a large board (at least 3' × 4') covered with black or black/blue flannel and a box of

assorted flannel pieces in various shapes and colors. The pieces are used to arrange settings and scenes on the flannel board that are needed to illustrate a story or play. Children can also use the board to invent games or play traditional games such as Tic-Tac-Toe.

10. *Set up a block or auto city or a race car track.* Again, a predesigned floor mat keeps this activity contained.

11. *Have pretend telephone conversations.* Make available two real phones that don't work anymore. Children will do the rest.

12. *Write notes to a friend using a manual typewriter.* Students put the notes in a real mailbox to be distributed to classmates later.

13. *Play traditional bingo.* This old favorite needs no explanation.

5

Introducing the Green Creativity Corner

*Let me have a few minutes at a roomy table
with lots of supplies to build, draw, cut, paste, create,
and display things. Now that's fun!*

Who Is the Green Creativity Corner For?

A good creativity corner can captivate the imaginations of many children at once. What a treat it can be! It will fascinate and attract the artistic children who love to express themselves with colorful, satisfying designs, decorations, doodles, and sketches. They are often crafts oriented and love the smell of school paste and glue sticks.

These are the children who sketch and doodle designs in the margins of their papers. A give-away trait: Their book covers, notebooks, pencil boxes (and sometimes fingernails, arms, and legs) are decorated. Is this description reminding you of anyone in your class? If so, jot down their names for further observation. These children seem most comfortable with scissors, pencils, or markers in their hands. Their desktops (and desks) are often a mess with erasure debris, pencil marks, crayon wax, and marker overrun. They are often enthusiastic children who concentrate any spare class time on creating, designing, sketching, and such. Because they like to work up until the very last free minute, the insides of their desks often look like a frustrated artist's studio.

What Do Creative Children Appreciate?

It is really fun to offer a classroom utopia to creative children. Their level of appreciation and delight is very rewarding. To locate the best space, head for the sink or wet area. Carpeted areas are risky. A big rectangular table that can handle four to six chairs is ideal. If you have space to accommodate a nearby round table with four additional chairs and (bonus) an art easel (for use with newsprint, crayons, and markers), all the better. Because you do not want this area to be overcrowded, you will want to set a cap on the number of children who can be in the corner at one time. Once you decide on the number, post it clearly and stick to it. If the area cannot accommodate all interested children, consider introducing a "sign-up" chart to reserve space for the next indoor recess.

Add a Display Area

The creativity area also needs some display space. An obvious one is a nearby bulletin board with a permanent caption such as, "Celebrating Ms. Miller's Artists." If no bulletin board is nearby, consider a roll of tape and a designated area of painted wall. Ideally, another display area would be available for three-dimensional objects (such as clay figures, origami projects, and shadow boxes). I have also seen very effective additional display spaces made by stretching a clothesline across an area and offering a box of colorful plastic clothespins. In any case, the display area can provide a way for each artist to be celebrated.

How to Encourage Independence, Cooperation, and Responsibility

The children need to know that to use the creativity corner, certain agreements must be honored. For instance, this corner requires sharing both space and supplies. It also requires respecting the creations of others. Displaying work should be an option, not a requirement, and finally, these artistic children must be willing to stop, clean up, and return to their seats by the final bell. Work that is still "in progress" can be taken home at the end of the day for completion.

Learning bonus: Being recognized for special talents and being encouraged by a thoughtful teacher to create can boost children's courage to take risks in areas where they have less confidence and skill.

What Do Creative Children Love to Do?

The activities that follow are divided into three general categories: activities that invite children to build and invent, to draw, color, and cut, and to create with writing.

Question to ask: Will this activity entice the children to use their imagination to create something?

Activities That Invite Building and Invention

1. Build a block tower.

2. Build a Lincoln Log™ fort.

3. Make pipe cleaner people; put them in a diorama village (perhaps connected with a social studies unit).

4. Make an origami object (an idea book can be both helpful and inspiring).

5. Build a clay figure. Label it and display it.

6. Create a mobile. Test it out.

Activities That Invite Drawing, Coloring, and Cutting

7. Color a picture at the easel (as opposed to paints, which can take too long for the recess period).

8. Color a picture and convert it into a puzzle. Challenge a friend to put it together.

9. Sketch from artists' "how-to" books such as how to draw cartoons, horses, cats, dogs, cars, or people.

Activities That Invite Creating With Writing

10. Write or type a story and illustrate it. Bind the book and design the cover.

11. Play with a printing set. Write notes in a secret code to friends. Decorate the envelopes and slip the notes in their desks. Make one for the teacher.

12. Make up clues for a treasure hunt. Hide the clues. Try it yourself first. Invite a friend to try it.

13. Create a special card or stationery for a friend. Use the stamp set.

6

Establishing the Blue Quiet Corner

*Ahhh, for a calm, safe place to relax, read a book,
or work a puzzle with a friend.*

Who Is the Blue Quiet Corner For?

In every active classroom there is the need for a quieter area that is set aside from the main traffic paths. This is a peaceful, calming area of the room that is equipped for relaxing with an interesting book, puzzle, magazine, or some other quiet pursuit. However, don't be fooled by the title. The quiet corner is not only for shy, quiet, and reserved children. If that were the case, it could be a very lonely corner. In fact, you may be surprised by the children who would be attracted to a calm area that looks inviting for reading, relaxing, and doing low-key activities that require some concentration such as word games, crossword puzzles, chess, and checkers.

The Location and Setup

Look again at your classroom floor plan and locate a good spot for this area. Ideally, it will be located in a corner so the walls on two sides can offer some peace and quiet from the action. The best corners will have something that delineates the other two sides as well. It makes the area seem separate and cozy. Even though tempting, you should not consider tents or tepees unless they are constructed of heavy transparent plastic. I have seen such plastic available by the yard in department stores where self-adhesive papers and oilcloth are sold. Opaque structures can provide too much privacy, which could interfere with a child's safety or your function of classroom oversight. Also, provide as much distance as you can from the high-activity areas.

Activity Ideas for the Quiet Zone

When selecting activities for this area, consider a goal of about 90 choices. The selections should fill up about three bins. One sure way to make this corner boring is to skimp on choices. The activity of browsing through a generous supply of materials before making a selection is part of the fun at this corner. Consider the following:

1. Collect 15 to 30 books and create a "book nook." (You might also have a class contest to name the book nook, if you like.) Include books that can be completed in 20 to 30 minutes or that can be enjoyed in one sitting, such as children's magazines, classic comics, choose your own adventure stories, mysteries, short stories, poetry, an

interesting-looking dictionary, picture dictionaries, and several above-grade-level readers with the grade levels clearly marked on the spine. (This will be a major hit!) Another great thing to add, if you have room, is a set of used encyclopedias. You can often find these at yard sales, or you can request one in the church bulletin, community paper, or in a note that goes home with the students. You may want the "book nook" to be available for instructional times too. In that case, collect some of the best recess reading, color-code them with blue dots, and put them into a special bin. Direct the monitors to bring out the bin just for indoor recess. The color coding helps everyone know which materials are to be returned. Note: In many schools, you can borrow 15 to 30 books from the media center for use in your book nook. Then, every month, you can exchange them for a new collection. This ensures that you always have a fresh supply of books.

2. Gather word puzzle magazines, mazes, crosswords, and so on. The puzzle pages can be placed in separate plastic protectors, completed with water-based markers, and then erased for future use. On the back, an answer sheet can be placed with a listing of students who have completed the puzzle along with the date. (About 30 puzzle pages would provide great variety and could be easily stored in a second bin with room to spare.)

3. Add four or five challenging jigsaw puzzles. These could be completed on the floor or on top of a student's desk.

4. Offer taped stories that can be completed in 15 or 20 minutes. The stories could be taped by parents or purchased commercially. A set of earphones would make a great addition.

5. Add a few games of concentration such as chess, checkers, and scrabble that could be played at desks if activity tables are not available.

6. Save old toy catalogs to peruse. It may sound amazing, but children enjoy window shopping too.

7. Laminate "find Waldo" pictures and other hidden picture puzzles.

8. Collect books of jokes and riddles.

9. Add a couple copies of the *Guiness Book of World Records*.

10. Finally, add two world globes for "in search of" contests (you will also need an egg timer or minute-minder). This game may surprise you with its popularity. Print the names of continents, oceans, major countries, island groups, and special land features (such as famous mountains and rivers) on strips of paper. I prefer to color-code each category. Laminate the strips. Do not limit the strips to easy places just because the children are younger. Let them decide what they can do. For lower grades, just keep the print big enough for easy reading. The children take turns challenging each other to locate the sites.

7

Designating the Red "Time-Away" Corner

How did I get in trouble with everybody? I wish I could just get away for a few minutes and start all over!

Who Is the Red Time-Away Corner For?

The time-away corner is for any child who is temporarily unable or unwilling to comply with the agreed-on standards of behavior to the point that someone's safety is jeopardized or the play of other children is disrupted. The time-away corner is for the child who is careening out of control and needs a safe place to "pull over" before he or she gets in an accident. The red corner is not meant to be a place of punishment. Rather, it is meant to offer a safe haven where an overwrought child can rest, calm down, or perhaps even take a nap. Then, when the child feels in charge of himself or herself again, he or she is free to rejoin friends.

Use of the Corner

Children should not be sent to the red corner unwillingly and then forgotten for the entire recess period. However, the teacher can ask a child, who is obviously having a bad day and disturbing all those around, to go to the time-out corner for a number of minutes. A visit to the corner can also be self-imposed. Visitors to the red corner are asked to sign a log and enter the number of "get-away" minutes they feel they need or have been charged by the teacher. A timer can be set to let them know when they may return to play.

The Location and Setup

The red corner should be as far away from the crowd as possible but still be in view of the teacher. It should offer some privacy and be equipped for rest, calm, writing, reading, thinking, and perhaps listening to calming music on headphones. If possible, the lighting should be softer; the area should be carpeted and include a comfortable chair such as a rocker or beanbag. The area should connote peace and comfort as opposed to a place of punishment, which is often the purpose of time-away areas. This is not the case here. The message is that it is not bad to be in the time-away area. Sometimes it can be necessary to get away from others for a few minutes to think and regain control. In fact, it is commendable to know oneself well enough to say, "I need to get away for a few minutes."

Of course, there are times when the student will not self-select to go to the time-away area. The visit will be entirely teacher directed. In such cases, the message to the student should be that sometimes our behavior signals to others that we are temporarily not in control. When this occurs, the teacher is required to take action that protects the rights and safety of others. The students and their parents need to know in advance that when the children lose control, they will be asked to leave the play area and retreat to the red corner.

What Do Distraught Children Appreciate?

Children who are not in control of themselves usually know it, even if they can't admit it. They appreciate the teacher who understands that this can happen to anyone, and that it doesn't mean they are bad children. It helps to keep in mind that the child isn't having any fun during these times either. Children who have lost their self-control can worry that they will never feel in control again. They are encouraged by the teacher who holds on to the image of them as good when they have temporarily lost it themselves.

Upset children appreciate not being embarrassed in front of their friends and classmates and not being yelled at. In fact, everyone in the class, school, and at home appreciates teachers who do not yell or raise their voices in anger. Even though other students may not be involved, knowing that the adult is angry (and maybe out of control as well) is a very frightening thing to a child. Ironically, yelling and embarrassing a child publicly can also create peer support for the child being yelled at. It can demonstrate to the class that the adult cannot be trusted. Tomorrow they may be the recipient of the yelling or anger.

Guidelines for Use

If an offense has occurred that has hurt or infringed on the rights of another, the child may be asked to come up with a plan regarding how he or she will follow up on what has occurred. That might consist of writing a note to someone or a letter of confession to the principal, teacher, child, or parent.

8

Creating and Implementing

an Automatic Pilot System

Creating Systems and Routines
That Make It Easy to Be Good

Let's take stock. We have arranged the classroom, packed it with great activities, and identified some core standards of conduct. Now what? How do we unleash all this activity without having chaos reign for 20 to 30 minutes? The answer lies in the thoughtful creation of systems and routines that will enable the children to act responsibly and independently. We need to create an automatic pilot system and then patiently train the children in its use. The bonus for the teacher will be that not only will indoor recess become a snap, but the management of regular classroom instruction will improve as well.

Creating effective classroom systems and routines is one of those invisible skills that great teachers have. It is invisible because if you step into their classrooms after mid-

September or so, you are struck with the calm, orderly, and productive movement of busy children. Where is their chaos? The teachers don't seem to be doing hardly anything to get this great behavior out of the children. Is this fair? You can bet that this teacher was proactive in August and early September to develop and train the children in the use of effective systems and routines. By October, all you see is the beautiful, well-deserved result. The class can function almost automatically. How did it get that way?

What Is a Routine?

Simply put, effective classroom routines are habits that children have been intentionally taught that enable them to move around the room freely with purpose, make good decisions, work cooperatively with others, and perform their tasks while maintaining a safe, orderly, and fun learning environment.

What Is a System?

A recess management system consists of many learned routines. Some of the recess routines will serendipitously overlap with instruction time. For instance, the standards of class conduct are likely to be the same for both recess and instruction.

Designing classroom management systems can be fun to create and to teach. Also, children love to join in to "test" new routines and give their feedback. Their perspective is invaluable for helping to identify trouble spots. This is especially true if you are inexperienced in developing such systems.

Developing Smooth and Efficient Management Systems

Here's how it works:

1. Think about your vision for indoor recess. Ahhhh! Make it great! Then, identify what you want the children to do. (Example: Begin and end recess in an orderly way.)

2. Do your best to think like the children. You may want to go sit in a student's desk and look around the room. Are there reminders, labels, posters, and cues? Are there helpful aids for the forgetters? What questions might come to a child's mind?

3. Ask yourself, "What do the children need to know, and what must they be able to do to make the recess work well?" A good way to find out is to anticipate what you can and then observe the next recess with pencil and clipboard in hand. Note what problems are occurring. What questions do you hear more than twice? Jot down observations.

4. Learn from your observations and be willing to refine the system. Does something need to be changed, added, removed, or clarified? Do not accept that the problem is "just the children" and give up. The problem is most likely to be a systems flaw that can be corrected once it is identified. It is rarely the children. They just want to have a fun recess. If the solution eludes you, consider involving the children in problem solving or asking a colleague to observe.

The Indoor Recess System in Action

1. The "Pre-recess" Preparation Steps

▶ The teacher informs the students that it will be an indoor recess day.
▶ The Indoor Recess Contract is posted and reviewed. Other pertinent agreements are reviewed.

▶ The children are reminded to go straight to their seats when they return to the classroom for dismissal by table to play areas.

▶ If there were any problems last time, the children are reminded of the new agreements.

▶ The monitors are reminded of their roles for setting up the areas for play.

▶ Students are also reminded that cleanup begins when they hear the Lone Ranger theme and that everyone must be in their seat, reading a book or journaling, by the last note!

2. The Launch Plan

▶ The children come back from lunch and go straight to their seats, as previously instructed.

▶ The recess monitors (three students who have volunteered to act as the "setup team," one serving each center) place the color-coded bins in the areas. The teacher has given this rotating team of volunteers a "tour of their duties" ahead of time. They are clear as to their role. As a reward, once setup is complete, the monitors may go to the area of their choice.

▶ The teacher dismisses one or two tables where children are demonstrating that they are ready to play by their rapt attention.

▶ As soon as possible, other tables are dismissed, and a 20-minute timer is set.

▶ Students are free to enjoy the activities of their choice for the full 20 minutes.

3. Ending Indoor Recess

▶ The timer dings.

▶ The teacher begins playing the Lone Ranger theme to signal 3 minutes are remaining, and the closure process is under way. Students playing games take their last turns, construction and creative projects are stopped, and everyone begins cleanup.

▶ A few students return to their desks. If there is a class puzzle posted on the board, they may get busy to see if they can solve it.

▶ The music gradually gets louder until the final note is played. STOP! With this final flourish of activity, recess is now officially over. (If this is during the implementation phase, the teacher might offer a grab bag prize to the first, third, and sixth persons to be seated.) Note: The grab bag idea can also be used on a random basis to reinforce the routines throughout the year.

4. Transitioning Back to Instruction

To complete the transition back to instruction, the teacher needs to be "ready to go" as soon as recess is over, with a clear, crisp direction for instruction. It helps the visual learners if the direction is also written on the board. For best success here, the teacher needs to capitalize on this brief window of whole class attention. If the teacher has to stop and talk to someone, go find a book on the back table, or in any way "leave the scene," the opportunity for a smooth transition to instruction is compromised. Children are quick to pick up on lack of teacher leadership here and can be ruthlessly impatient.

Consider that the class must be productively engaged within 1 to 2 minutes. Because that is not always possible, it is a good idea to have a few emergency "transition activities" that can be pulled out on a moment's notice when you need to buy some time. In the old days, it was called, "Everyone put your heads down on the desk and rest for 2 minutes!" We can probably come up with better transition activities now, but you have to admit, that technique demonstrated decision making and leadership.

A Great Transition Activity: The Tangram Challenge

Preparing the Activity

1. To be ready with this transition activity on a moment's notice, you will need to do some advance preparation: Prepare a box of 35 tangram-like puzzles (or one for each student). The puzzles can be handmade on stiff, colored paper, laminated, and stored in Ziploc bags.

2. Next, prepare a large poster showing a tantalizing tangram animal or design. A batch of a dozen or so of these laminated posters would make a great collection. (If you prefer, the challenges could be put on overhead transparencies instead of posters.)

3. Keep these supplies in a safe place near your desk for quick access.

4. Instruct the indoor recess monitors in advance as to their role in the quick setup for this activity.

Setting the Activity in Motion

Now you are set! When you need transition help, simply post the tangram challenge where everyone can see it, signal the recess monitors to go into action distributing the individual puzzles, and, if you wish, set a timer for 5 minutes. Now you can deal with an emergency, and the class is still under control. When you are ready to begin instruction, ask if anyone has solved the challenge. If so, award the student (or first two to three students) a grab in the grab bag.

Finally, the indoor recess monitors collect the puzzles and return them to the proper place to be ready for the next emergency.

Can You Find the Hidden Fox?

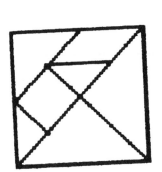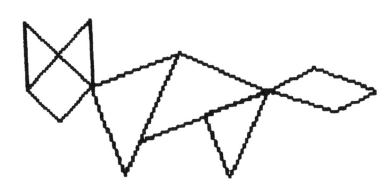

9

Adding Special Activity Areas

Suggestions for Special Areas

Once the basic plan is implemented, other special activity centers can be added over time. These centers are a little more involved to create, but if you have the room, they are worth it. Often, a generous parent or community member comes along who is willing to coordinate the construction of such a project for you. Just in case you get that lucky, here are suggestions for four ready ideas.

A Puppet Theater

Although a sturdy cardboard box can serve as a fine theater, the ideal is real plywood construction. Curtains that can open and close are an added plus. Once you get the theater, a few hand puppets are all you need to add a new dimension to indoor playtime. Imaginative students can invent short one-act plays that can later be shared for the entertainment of the whole class. An extra incentive is to advertise that the shows occasionally will be videotaped and that the video can be borrowed to show at home.

A Classroom Movie Theater

This center doesn't require special construction. The needs are more for space and equipment. All you need is some space in an area that is a little darker, a television equipped with a video player, a collection of about 10 (one for each month) short videos such as cartoons, and some nice fat floor pillows. A limited number of "tickets" could be available to ensure that this center does not get overcrowded.

A Computer Center

Most classrooms are equipped now with computers. Because there is never time to play computer games during the school day, this would make a great recess activity.

Students would probably love to make recommendations regarding favorite games to be offered. Student volunteers might provide the perfect introduction and commercial for this area as well. Once you try incorporating computer games, you might find that some extra agreements need to be made regarding the use of this center.

A Production Stage and Costume Trunk

This center also calls for some special construction, but it is not necessarily out of the question if you have a small classroom. The "stage" could be as simple as a special rug (about 3' × 4') that is unrolled to designate the area. The main ingredient is a trunk (or large box) that contains interesting hats, shoes, jackets, dresses, a feather boa, canes, handbags, a briefcase, a pipe, a mustache, wigs, hairpieces, a football jersey, animal masks, a black cape, and so on. The idea is to spark the imagination of pretending directors, playwrights, actors, and actresses. If you have a book of simple plays, great. If not, with a trunk like this, you will have some soon.

10

Keeping Indoor Recess Fresh and Fun

We all know that children love surprises, special days, and new things. The teacher and students can have some extra fun during indoor recess by introducing a new game or play idea once a month. Once introduced, the new game is added to the other play choices for the rest of the year. Of course, at the end of the year, when the teacher inventories all the games, the 12 special activities should be removed to a separate box for introduction all over again to next year's class. That's when all the work you are doing now will really pay off.

A Month-by-Month Collection of Surprises and Curiosities

☆ *September: Can You Solve My Hidden-Word Puzzle?*

It is nearly impossible to keep a supply of good puzzle sheets around. However, you don't have to if you teach students to make their own. Students can challenge each other to solve their puzzles. For extra fun, a class record can be started that invites breaking. If you get this kind of challenge going on, you could be set for the year.

Materials Needed

Students will need copies of the blank hidden-word puzzle on the next page. They will also need access to crayons, pencils, erasers, rulers, and a dictionary. You will need to create a large class poster for the record setters. (Note: The poster could be laminated for use next year.)

Directions

1. Students are directed to come up with a puzzle theme—for example, Jungle Prowlers, Favorite Colors, Things That Roll, Unsinkables, What You Never Want to See on Your Plate, Baseball Stars, and so on.

2. Students think of 15 or so fun words that fit the category and list them in the word box. (It is a good idea to get a spell check on the words too.) They might want to enhance their puzzles with a drawing on the borders or at the bottom of the page.

3. Next, they decide where they want to feature each word on the puzzle. Words can be placed horizontally, vertically, or diagonally. Using a ruler, they draw a light pencil line through the right number of boxes as a guide.

4. After that, they print the word in the boxes, one letter at a time.

5. Now they are ready to challenge a daring classmate. Winners get to sign up on the posted class record.

Guidelines for Use

Duplicate about 200 copies of the blank puzzle page. Introduce the idea to the whole class during language arts time on a rainy day. Let the students try one as a class activity. Once introduced, put the blank puzzles in a specially marked bin in the quiet corner and invite them to begin setting a class record at recess.

Hidden Word Puzzle

Created by _____

Directions:

To make your own hidden word puzzle, first write down the list of words you wish to hide on the lines below. You might choose words all about one topic or theme such as "jungle words." Next choose a straight line on the puzzle where you will print your first word (print one letter in each box.) You may go across, down, backwards, or diagonally on the line. Next, choose a line to write your second word. Continue to write all the words. Last, add other letters to all the missing boxes to hide your words. Now, challenge a friend to solve your puzzle. Good luck!

List your hidden words here:

_____ _____ _____ _____
_____ _____ _____ _____
_____ _____ _____ _____
_____ _____ _____ _____
_____ _____ _____ _____
_____ _____ _____ _____

Novak, D. *Help! It's An Indoor Recess Day!* © 2000. Corwin Press, Inc.

☆ *October: Create a Treasure Hunt*

A consistently popular activity center with children is the treasure hunt. It consists of a clue written on a strip of paper that is left in a "treasure chest." The treasure seeker follows the direction on the clue, which leads to yet another written clue. The hunt goes through four or five more clues before the "treasure" is finally reached.

Materials Needed

A small box decorated as a treasure chest, scissors, paper, marking pens, an optional grab bag of prizes (see below).

A grab bag of prizes and treasures can increase the fun by providing real treasures. An investment in a bag of plastic squiggly worms, monsters, funny eraser tops, and rings like the ones dentists give away provides a year's supply of treasures. Each item can be gift wrapped and placed in a grab bag to give the creator of the treasure hunt a real prize to offer.

Directions

The teacher demonstrates to the class how to plan out a hunt, hide the clues, and then test the hunt to be sure it works before offering it as a challenge to a classmate.

Guidelines for Use

The directions for creating a treasure hunt should be written up in a little booklet that is kept in the bottom of the treasure box for reference.

☆ *November: Make a Jigsaw Puzzle*

Children select and cut out an interesting picture from a magazine, or they can draw and color a picture of their own. In either case, the picture is glued to stiff paper and then cut into a puzzle using sharp scissors. The pieces are kept in a signed puzzle envelope that the student can also make. When the puzzle is ready, the student can challenge a classmate to complete it before the salt runs out on a 3-minute egg timer.

Materials Needed

Students need access to magazines to cut up, scissors, glue, stiff paper, ruler, and a 3-minute egg timer.

Directions

The teacher demonstrates making a jigsaw puzzle to the entire class. The only problems children typically encounter include trying to cut the puzzle apart before the glue is dry or making the pieces too small to handle. Because the activity requires cutting and pasting, it needs to be done at the creativity center.

☆ *December: Connect-the-Dot Challenges*

This old-fashioned puzzle for two takes very little direction or materials. It makes a great indoor recess game because it takes up a minimum amount of storage space, requires very little room to play, and has an easy cleanup. It is probably best suited for the quiet corner but could also be played at desks located anywhere in the room.

Materials Needed

Students will need pencils and copies of the puzzle grid.

Directions

Students take turns connecting any two dots going in a vertical or horizontal direction. When a line forms a four-sided box, the person writes his or her initial in the box, thus earning one point. The person with the most points at the end of the game is the winner.

Guidelines for Use

Pages of the puzzle could be stored in a blue color-coded bin in the quiet corner. During the introduction, the teacher would explain where the puzzles are located. Students interested in playing would simply get the sheets as needed.

Dot-to-Dot Puzzle

Directions: Connect any two dots with a straight line. Whenever the line makes a closed box, you may write your initial in the box and receive one point. The player with the most points at the end of the game is the winner.

Player 1 _____ Final score_____
Player 2 _____ Final score_____

☆ *January: The Design Box*

This is so simple that you won't believe its popularity until you introduce it. It is based on the belief that, regardless of age, children love to produce beautifully colored pictures and designs. Once introduced, the design box can vary all year, and every year it can get more interesting. Over time, some things are bound to disappear, so don't be distressed—just build that fact into your plan. If special things are going to be offered that need a little supervision, put them in a smaller "sign-out" box.

Materials

Find an interesting-looking box that is large enough to hold the collection. Include fun items such as rubber stamps, geometric templates, several compasses, short plastic rulers, and realistic templates such as cardboard or plastic patterns for drawing animals, automobiles, motorcycles, ships, boats, planes, rockets, and so on. Also include about 100 pages that have been torn out of a variety of coloring books, lots of blank paper, and a variety of art media such crayons, wooden pencils, and fine-line felt markers.

Directions for Use

Instruct the students to look through the box, consider the possibilities, and invent designs. Compass designs may need to be demonstrated. Completed designs may be displayed on the design board for 1 week. These designs should include the artist's name and the date.

☆ *February: The Valentine Mailbox*

This activity gives students the opportunity to create special Valentine cards for friends and then "mail them" by placing the completed cards in a classroom mailbox for later distribution.

Materials

A plastic bin containing bits and pieces of construction paper, wrapping paper, metallic papers, glitter (if you are really brave), glue sticks, scissors, crayons, wooden pencils, felt-tipped markers, and some samples of Valentines. You will need a country-style mailbox as well.

Directions

Once given the idea and shown the supplies in the bin, students don't need a lot of instruction. For added excitement, the art teacher could be invited to discuss some ideas about commercial card design, including developing a personal trademark for the back of the card.

Guidelines for Use

This activity would be a great addition to the creativity center. Also, for the month of February, a volunteer team of students could serve as the mail carriers to distribute the Valentine mail at some designated point in the day.

☆ *March: Secret Coded Messages*

Many children love the mystery of secret coded messages. This activity should include a couple of examples of codes and a coded message that says something such as, "Go to the chalkboard. Draw a box. Write your name in it. The teacher will give you a surprise."

Materials

This activity is recommended for the quiet corner. You will need a plastic bin with a blue sticker on it that includes the following: one or more secret codes printed on stiff paper that have been laminated or placed in a plastic sleeve, sample messages that have been written in the code, and blank paper for making up new messages. A great addition would be a paperback book on secret codes.

Directions

Demonstrate the fun by giving everyone a copy of a secret coded message in the morning. Post the code on a large poster or overhead projector. At the end of the day, ask for a student volunteer to read the message. Invite students to try their hand during the next indoor recess.

Guidelines for Use

This activity would make a great contribution to the quiet corner. Put all the needed materials in a blue color-coded bin. In the introduction, let the children know where the bin will be located.

☆ *April: The Hands-On Box*

This is a box of all kinds of three-dimensional puzzles. It includes things such as interlocking metal puzzles, wooden cubes and shapes, plastic Rubik Cubes, and other puzzles that require manipulation and hands-on solution finding.

This box may not be for all children, but for lovers of puzzles, it is a dream!

Materials

Almost any three-dimensional puzzle is a candidate for this box. The more variety the better. Craft fairs, hobby shops, and sidewalk sales make good bets for locating these puzzles.

Directions

The teacher only needs to give children a peek inside to motivate them for this activity. The best location for the hands-on box would be the Yellow Action Corner.

☆ *May: Be the Teacher*

A lot of children love playing with duplicates of old classroom worksheets. Other fun things that can be added to this bin would be a couple of red marking pencils and a few stamps with statements such as "Good Work," "Great Job," and "Try Again." You can also add stamps that have smiley faces and blue ribbons. Add extra challenge to this activity by including a copy of the 100 most misspelled words and some lined quiz paper.

Materials

Save copies of extra worksheets throughout the year. For extra interest, ask next year's teacher for some contributions. Put those sheets in a special container labeled "Above Grade Level." Do the same thing with worksheets from lower grades. Children love to do very easy worksheets that remind them how proficient they are becoming. Add a collection of rubber stamps and a couple of stamp pads as described above.

Directions

To introduce this activity, the teacher only needs to inform the students where the bin is located. This activity is best located in the active area of the classroom. If it can be located in close proximity to the chalkboard, then all the better.

☆ June: Create a Summer Mural

Usually, there are few indoor recess periods during the month of June. However, here is an idea just in case. If you wish, the notion of creating a mural could be adapted for any other month as well.

Materials

The materials required for this activity are usually on hand. You will need an 8-foot span of rolled bulletin board paper or butcher paper, markers, crayons, several scissors, old magazines, and glue sticks. The idea is for the students to create a scene showing a place they would love to go over the summer. They place themselves somewhere in the picture. The whole class might vote on the vacation site when the activity is introduced. Examples of scenes would include a mountain scene, beach scene, dude ranch, foreign country, Disney World, and so on. An artistic parent or the art teacher might make up the basic scene for students to add to.

Directions

Students are invited to study the scene and select where they would be located in it. They draw themselves on a separate paper and then place themselves in the scene. If they wish, they can add items to make the scene real, such as trees, houses, and so on, that are cut from magazines or hand drawn. If it can be arranged for students to have pictures of themselves, they can have fun pasting their heads on bodies cut from magazines. The mural stays up for the entire month to be added to as time permits. For extra fun, students can add cartoon conversation bubbles that contain witty statements and humorous lines.

Celebrating Success: A Photo Album for Parents Night

A great way to recognize children who are following the new indoor recess standards for safe and cooperative play is to take an "action shot" of them during indoor recess time.

The photos can be displayed in a special album on "back to school" night or during American Education Week. The beginning page of the album could include a copy of the class standards for indoor play surrounded by a colorful border. Each student could be invited to sign the page indicating his or her support for the standards using colored pens. The teacher should make sure that every child is represented in at least one of the photos.

Final Thoughts

When I think of the many generous adults who successfully manage classrooms full of exuberant elementary-age children during indoor recess (and have fun doing it), I imagine creative and talented teachers, classroom assistants, principals, and parent volunteers with great senses of humor. They are ageless and are renewed and entertained by watching children at play.

There is no doubt in my mind that the successful management of indoor recess is an accomplishment that takes great skill in organization, management, imagination, leadership, and diplomacy. Most teachers will agree that it is much harder to manage children during free playtime than during more structured classroom times.

There is also a great deal of valuable information that can be gained about individual children by observing them during free play. Some of this information includes the following:

▶ Insights into the child's strategies for interacting with peers

▶ Information about social patterns, cliques, popularity, acceptance, and rejection

▶ Evidence of the child's ability or willingness to follow directions

▶ Valuable information regarding learning styles and preferences

▶ Information regarding personal confidence, decision making, follow-through, and personal organization

▶ Validation of classroom observations regarding persistence to task and attention span

Finally, I believe that indoor recess gives educators, both new and experienced, the unique opportunity to experiment with classroom systems and design a plan that will motivate, refresh, and intrigue children. It is the one time when we don't have to limit ourselves to a prescribed curriculum or "learning outcome." We can revive our old play instincts and set our unabashed goal: create fun! I believe this experience can bring out the little bit of Walt Disney that is probably hiding in most good elementary teachers.

I wish you the very best of luck with your plans. I hope that you will be intrigued enough to try some of the ideas that have been described. I invite you to take a few minutes and share your experiences with me. I would enjoy hearing from you!

CORWIN
PRESS

The Corwin Press logo—a raven striding across an open book—represents the happy union of courage and learning. We are a professional-level publisher of books and journals for K-12 educators, and we are committed to creating and providing resources that embody these qualities. Corwin's motto is "Success for All Learners."